Tea Time with
GOD

Stories to Encourage Her

A WOMAN'S DEVOTIONAL

Tammy L. White

AUTOGRAPH

TEA TIME WITH GOD

A Phenomenal Women's Series, Volume I

Tammy L. White

Copyright © 2016 by Tammy L. White

Printed in the United States of America

ISBN: 978-0692802427

Library of Congress Control Number: 2016918363

Cover Photo by: Tyia Mills Photography

Back Photo by: Restless Wings Photography

Editing, Formatting, and Proofreading by:

SD Horton Enterprises

P.O. Box 1612

Alamogordo, NM 88311

www.sdhortonenterprises.com

TABLE OF CONTENTS

Introduction

Tea Time With God, is meant to be a devotional for women who want a closer and deeper relationship with God. The real life experiences in the book will allow women to relate and connect on another level. Being able to relate to real life circumstances and watching God unveil His purpose and plan in so many instances will be encouraging. Regardless of your struggle at work, home, or church, you will be able to see God's hand in the life of the writer and experience God for yourself as you hold on to your faith in Christ.

A note from the Author...

I'm excited about what God is doing right now in the lives of His people. My heart for women and the desire to see them persevere, grow, conquer, and win, is the reason this devotional is a series. Watch God show His unmerited, underserved favor in my life in such a way that brings peace to the reader and greater intimacy with God on a personal level. You will get to see the lives of a few other women and their challenges and triumph as you walk through this first volume of Tea Time with God. So ladies, grab a cup tea and relax. Devote this time in prayer and fellowship with God. Pray for me, pray for the writers, pray for the women in our families, and seek God for yourself in the very place you are. I promise, He will meet you where you are, with your cup of tea in hand and overflowing blessings like you never imagined!

FOREWORD

What a joy to see that this thing that has been in Tammy's heart for so long has come to pass. Friends are great; you're able to look back and see how lives have been lived out before God. Tammy's life was never easy, but all the time I watched as she would hold on to God and just trust in His word. It's been a blessing to watch her raise her family in line with God's word and see how God has so blessed her. Tammy's life is just another example of what God can do if we would walk upright before Him. Tammy has always had a heart to reach out to help others, from the young women in Hawaii to the women in Washington state to encourage and be an example of God's love. We all need encouragement sometimes. I'm certain that many will be blessed through this work. This is one of those times where you can feel it in your spirit that something good is about to happen.

Pastor Offie S. Sheard, III
Baltimore, Maryland, USA

iv

DEDICATION

This book is dedicated to all the women out there who struggle with their relationship with God, but are working hard to find that place of solace. Throughout my struggles with relationships, especially with men, I noted that a relationship with God would allow me to understand why some life events had taken place. I would also like to dedicate this book to those who continue to support me and my growth in Christ and my endeavors like never before. Women across the globe have supported my zeal and tenacity when it comes to the things of Christ. This book is dedicated to those who have allowed me to speak into their lives, who have sought me out for prayer because of the light of Christ in my life, and those who continue to support me regardless of my past, as they accept my present. This book is dedicated to those who know that I am not perfect, but they love me anyway. This book is dedicated to those who strive to be a part of my life even though I tend to be so busy, or forget to follow up. This book is dedicated to those who love me and stand by me with support and excitement as they see my life unfold. You all know who you are and I love you.

SECTION ONE
-WHEN YOU LEAST EXPECT IT-

CHAPTER ONE

YOU NEVER KNOW

"For I know the thoughts that I think toward you, says the Lord, thoughts of peace and not of evil, to give you a future and a hope."

Jeremiah 29:11

A few years ago, I walked into one of those Rent-To-Own places to look for some furniture for short-term rental. I was greeted by a couple of the representatives who were very helpful and I made my selection pretty quick. The representative who was finalizing my purchase was very polite, very professional, and there was something about him; something I would describe as peculiar. He was explaining all the terms for the rental and making small talk about my needs and my options and I noticed that I really was not paying attention to anything he was saying because I was intrigued by him for some reason. I said to him, "Sidney you are a believer, right? " He smiled and said, "As matter fact I stopped going to church a while ago after my father died." I have to be honest with you Phenomenal women who are reading this, I cannot recall the entire reason why Sidney stop going to church, but I do recall that his father was a Preacher. Well my next words were, "Sidney my brother I want to encourage you, God has called you to a dynamic work in the kingdom, I think you are running and you need to go back." Sidney asked me how can I tell that he was a believer. I told him that we are different, we are a peculiar people I just knew that he a had connection and relationship with God. The spirit of discernment it is always at work.

I say all of this to tell you the end result, the praise report about Sidney. Shortly, very shortly I can tell you maybe a week or so later, Sidney contacted me on Facebook and told me not only had he gone back to fellowship with other believers, you know the saints of the Highest God, but he also started playing the keyboard for church again. Yes, he is also a musician and singer who was a Minister of Music at his previous church. He reported that he found a church home and continues to do ministry in the Olympia/Lacey area of Washington State.

You never know who you might run into or how you might impact their lives. God is always ready to use us; we just have to position ourselves to be used. It warms my heart to see him doing outreach, feeding the homeless, and functioning in ministry like never before. Everything sparked by the gift of discernment and the Holy Spirit at work! To God be the glory! Ladies allow God to use you! Make yourself available to Him daily.

SECTION TWO
-DO THE RIGHT THING-

CHAPTER TWO

COURAGE

"Trust in the Lord with all your heart, and lean not on your own understanding; In all your ways acknowledge Him and He will direct your paths."

Proverbs 3:5-6

Doing the right thing takes courage. Our expectations far outweigh reality or actuality. I am finding that courage shows up in too many comfort zones. I don't think we know what that word really means. Don't mistake your complacency for courage. They are not even distant relatives; they are bitter enemies. Just remember, when you make that courageous decision, be mindful to put your trust in God and consult with Him so you can make that courageous and victorious decision.

CHAPTER THREE

THE NEXT LEVEL

"But seek first the kingdom of God and His righteousness, and all these things shall be added to you."

Matthew 6:33

Just thinking...how can I be the best I can be in any relationship, without pursuing more of my relationship with Christ? I've researched so many things to get my clients, friends, family, etc, to their next level. However, I must continue to research the Word to get me to the next level. **#conviction**

SECTION THREE
-WORK ON YOURSELF / I'M WORKING ON ME-

CHAPTER FOUR

ALL LIVES MATTER IN CHRIST

What a chore it is to hear about innocent lives being taken! Today, as I spoke with my eldest son who has had to endure the reality of the challenges that his mother is facing, I inquired about the frustration I heard in his voice. Thinking that his frustrations were mainly about my situations and recent burdens with pain and injury, he said, "I'm tired of hearing about black unarmed men being killed by the police."

As he wears his "Black Lives Matter" shirt to work today, I'm wondering what's next. He's discouraged about folks saying, "When there are no laws in place regarding racial injustice in South Carolina and the confederate flag flies high with the anthem of devaluing black lives, I'm troubled," (paraphrased). As a Political Science grad from UW a year ago, his intentions and plans for law school raise another concern. The concern is, in my opinion, the judicial system does not support nor does it advocate all human lives. He has a voice and boy is he using it! We differ when it comes to protest, but we agree when it comes to our lives.

I still remain steadfast and faithful to the only one true and living God. While we lift our voices let words of prayer escape as well. We have power, sure we do. But we are a mere vapor without the presence and trust in God and the guidance of the Holy Spirit. You know what happens to vapors? They dissipate. So let God be true and EVERY man a lie when it comes to HIS plan and perfect will. I love all, but I don't fall into the traps of the deception. Simply because you are nice, but a part of a religious sect or culture that seeks to destroy others...I should embrace you and your doctrine? Not so! I should love you, but I don't have to subject my life to you.

If you don't believe in my God, fine I'm ok with that until you become judgmental while addressing my beliefs and faith directly. There is nothing anyone can do to stop my faith as a result of my relationship with Christ. One day we will all face Him, some in judgement, some embraced as His children. The point is, get it straight now so when HIS judicial system kicks in, you are acquitted! I'm working on me; how about you?

CHAPTER FIVE

NO SEPARATION HERE

Most of those who know me, know that I'm not a huge fan of politics. This whole separation of Church and State has me conflicted most of the time. How does one acknowledge God in all his or her ways for a directed path without consulting God even in political office? My love for people does not change when I make a decision not to agree with their lifestyle. I don't agree, you don't agree, we don't agree, that simple. As I'm working on me, I'm watching what's going on around me.

My life of repentance has just kicked up another notch. So with that, I'm just going to pray, be aware, knowing I'm not exempt because I trust God and my life can end in any fashion, today. At the end of the day ladies, folks have free-will, and that includes you and I. So as I exercise my right to serve Jesus, even though I have to watch where

I say His name because it's offensive to some, yet folks can use all the profanity in the world without giving it a second thought, I'm just going to pray about it. Same sex marriage is legal in 50 states, so what?! It does not change my "fundamentalist" Christian views as my son once stated. I love people, but I hate sin, even in my own life. So with that, I will not embrace anything against God. I can only manage me. Just know I firmly believe I cannot defeat God. So I'm on His side and trust me it's a wise decision and I'm on the winning team. What about you?

Devotion: Take some time during this election year to research Separation of Church and State. You will find that while it hints at the thought of protecting the American people, it stifles the acknowledgment of the only one true and living God when making decisions in public office. God allows officials to take office, please remember that. Laws are put in place and we must obey the law of the Land, however educate yourselves and pray for our country, **read (Romans 13:1-4).** There are exceptions to the rule in the eyes of God. You will find the peace that the word speaks of while you continue to serve God and acknowledge Jesus as Lord and Savior of your life. It is all a part of working on you. **Read: Philippians 4:6-7**

CHAPTER SIX

RE-FOCUSED

"Set your mind on things above, not on things on the earth. For you died, and your life is hidden with Christ in God."

Colossians 3:2-3

Many times in your journey you might feel like you are stagnant due to lack of focus. Recently due to lack of sleep this is how I felt. My commitment to re-focus is enough to encourage myself. My imperfections remind me of how much harder I must work on me. I live a repented lifestyle while serving a forgiving God. I'm encouraged and re-focused and encouraging you to do the same. I'm working on me, what about you? Be honest.

Devotion: Focus on the Scripture above. That 9pm Tea Time is calling your name. Spend some time with God over Tea. **Read: Colossians Chapter 3**

CHAPTER SEVEN

THE MIRROR TEST, LOOK IN AND LET GO!

"A good name is more desirable than great riches; to be esteemed is better than silver or gold."

Proverbs 22:1

Who are you representing? Are you doing it well? Yesterday I was listening to Dr. Charles Stanley of In-Touch Ministries and I was challenged to look into the mirror and ask myself, Tammy, how well are you representing Christ? The truth is, I've had a domino effect of life-altering, life-changing experiences this year, 2015. I have compromised on my convictions more often during those times while my faith continued to shift with my emotions. Dying to myself has to be the most difficult yet the most liberating exercise ever! I say exercise because it takes practice. Don't get me wrong, I've had some victories and have shattered some goals this year too. Ladies, you know what you need to do. The Holy Spirit has been nudging you and reminding you and ministering to you up to that very moment or act in your decision. There are a few things that I need to just **LET GO**, but the truth is I don't really want to **LET GO** and neither do you.

While we are being honest and transparent, we need to make that sound decision to just **LET GO!** It's because of that awful comfort zone. You know exactly what I'm talking about. It hurts to change; just admit it. God wants to use me and I will never know to what degree until I die to I. I don't want to look back on my life when I have less vigor and vitality with regrets about what God would have done and how it would have looked if I had just pressed and **LET GO!** Is that what you want to do, live with regrets? I don't think so. I think it's time for tea and to make that decision to **LET GO.**

Devotion: Make that decision to **LET GO** today. Grab your favorite tea, a quiet place and tell God all about it. You know what **IT** is. That relationship, **LET GO!** That anger, **LET GO!** That stronghold, **LET GO!** That habit, **LET GO!** The Holy Spirit is with us for comfort, strength, peace and guidance. Make some time for God today. Phenomenal Women, keep me in prayer as I take those steps to die to I and to **LET GO**. To all who are reading this right now, may you examine your life and live for Christ like never ever before! God bless you and take a longer look in that mirror today and do you know what, **LET GO!**

SECTION FOUR
-THERE IS NOTHING LIKE PEACE-

CHAPTER EIGHT

PURSUE PEACE

"You will keep him in perfect peace, whose mind is stayed on You, because he trusts in You."

Isaiah 26:3

Find that place where you had the most peace and make a visit. If you have to relocate, then do so!

Devotion: Make a habit of having some Tea Time with God. Take that time now. Many times when alone and in my own space, 9pm is my tea time. Grab some tea tonight. Reflect upon your day today. Think about those things that went well and give thanks to God. Think about those things that did not go so well and give thanks to God that you made it through. If you are still going though it, ask for guidance. Ask God what would He have you learn from this experience. Then sit quietly and listen to the Holy Spirit. Let God guide you and give you peace. Never make a decision without peace about that decision. Sit quietly, sip tea, and relax. Give it all to God; He cares. Make it a habit and watch how you handle life's demands. Give it to the Master. He specializes in making things right on our behalf.

Read: I Peter 5:6-7

SECTION FIVE
-DREAMS-

CHAPTER NINE

"SUFFER NO MORE"

2:15 am one morning, I awaken totally distraught because of a dream I was having.   Recently my uncle Arthur, my fishing buddy, my friend, my god-father had passed away on February 9, 2016. It was traumatic as my family was torn with division, anger, resentment, and bitterness about his death.

Well, without getting too much into the incidents surrounding his illness and death, just know I was in a deep sleep. In my dream this man was being hoisted onto a cross to be crucified. I could not see his face so the dream rewound like a missed scene in a movie.   The vision of this man's face became clear and the man being hoisted up was my uncle! He was being raised up on that cross as he hung almost lifeless. It took my breath away; and as I gasped for air, I woke up in tears.

First, I called my fiancé at the time and he noticed I was barely able to speak through my sobbing. He stated that he was on his way and I hung up the phone. I then felt compelled to text my best friend Theresa 3,000 miles away noting that it was after midnight her time. "Sis are you awake?" I texted. Her immediate answer was "yes!" Theresa called me, and through my sobbing I began to share the dream with her. She listened intently without speaking a word until I was done.

Knowing nothing prior to my revealing my dream, she said, "Tammy, I'm on YouTube watching the actor who played Jesus in The Passion of Christ and when you text me, he was explaining the suffering he endured when they hoisted him up onto the cross in the movie scene." That is where she stopped that video as I had text her with hopes that she was awake. Please note, Jesus was crucified by His own people. I will leave that right there. I know my uncle suffered, but no more! As my friend and I talked about this dream she texted me the link to the video. I began to watch it, and OMG! I stopped the video where he talked about really being ill during the filming and near actual death when being hoisted up on the cross. But he also said this..... they noted that he was ill and turned to Mel Gibson about continuing the filming after the 5th take. Mel asked him what he wanted to do and he said, "Just keep going. If I die while making this movie, more lives will be saved because of it!" Wow, wow, wow!

I stopped the video and called my friend back. I said, "Sis, who sent you this video?" She said, no one, it popped up on my screen out of the blue and I pressed play right before you called." My heart dropped, she said, "Now you understand how overwhelmed I was as I was listening because of what had just transpired prior to your text; I don't know what else to say." My uncle suffered, but no more. I know he is with The Lord. God cared so much that He set my sis in place strategically at that moment to minister to my troubled soul! Just know, there are no coincidences. God knows exactly what He is doing and who

He will use to minister to your troubled soul at the right time.

Phenomenal Women God loves you and He cares.

Here is the link: https://youtu.be/0Ejaw0F8-sY

SECTION SIX
-LEARNING TO STAND-

CHAPTER TEN

SHAKEN TO STABILITY

"Cast your cares on the Lord and He will sustain you; He will never let the righteous be shaken."

Psalm 55:22

If Psalm Chapter 55 verse 22 is true, why do we feel shaken at times when the Word states that we will not? "He will never let the righteous be shaken." Matthew Henry's commentary goes on to say this about being shaken; "He will never suffer the righteous to be moved; to be so shaken by any troubles, or their duty to God, or their comfort in Him. He will not suffer them to be utterly cast down. He, who bore the burden of our sorrows, desires us or our cares, that, as He knows what is best for us, he may provide it accordingly." How awesome is that?! Phenomenal Women, that is the scripture that comes to mind this very moment. As I sit on the side of my bed watching my youngest son going through another difficult moment in his life, I feel shaken. But when I stand on His word as I pray with my son, I realize that we don't have to carry those burdens and that's what this means. It means, "Why Tammy are you trying to do My job when I'm right here to see that you never have to because you are Mine." Wow!

So all of you whose hope is in Christ because by grace you were saved through faith (Ephesians 2:8) and everything was placed on the cross at Calvary, give it to God my sisters! Give every burden, every shortcoming, every doubt, every weight, every sin, every sickness, every issue, every stressor, every offense, every offender...give it ALL to Him. That is if you are righteous in His sight. Not when you look in the mirror but when you look at the cross. The question is, do you believe and have you received Him? If so, that burden/care certainly does not belong to you! Give it to Him. You know what time it is Phenomenal Woman! That's right, it's Tea Time.

CHAPTER ELEVEN

FAITH IN EVERY CIRCUMSTANCE

If you are the encourager, who encourages you when you need it? If you are the go-getter, who's going to get it for you when you can't? When you are feeling downtrodden because you are simply tired physically, mentally, emotionally and spiritually, you need prayer warriors in your life who know how to go to the throne of God on your behalf. That's who am to those who need a prayer warrior in their life. Iron sharpens iron, so prayer warriors keep me lifted up, I'm just tired and I know many of you are too, but be encouraged!

Read Psalm 27

SECTION SEVEN
-WHEN GOD SAYS YES-

CHAPTER TWELVE

IS DIVORCING REALLY THE OPTION?

"Commit your way to the Lord. Trust also in Him, and He shall bring it to pass."

Psalm 37:5

"You came to see me last night to tell me that you have decided to get a divorce. Last night I only listened, but this morning I woke up with a hope for you. For the past five years, I have been meeting with elders who have been married for 25+ years to get understanding from many perspectives as to what marriage and love is all about. Almost all the couples have said that at some point in their marriage they have stumbled upon inevitably difficult moments that called for a break. I spoke to one couple who had a few years apart only to re-discover their desire to grow old together and to do what was necessary to continue to deepen their love for one another. My hope for you is this, that you consider taking the route that some of our elders have taken in giving your marriage some space and time before the drastic decision of divorce. Answers to big questions need time to find lasting truth vs the truth of the moment. After this process the answer may be the same, but at least you will have the clarity to go about it all with certainty and integrity, but you may also find that spark that could save and rekindle your marriage."

-Jada Pinkett-Smith

While I'm not an advocate for breaks, I am an advocate for counseling and pausing before filing for divorce. I remember when I got married in 2005, God surrounded my husband and I with more than 25 couples who had been married for 20+ years. Each with a different story about how they made it, but the similarity was that they all wanted the marriage to work. If one does not want the marriage to work, there is nothing the other can do. Other than pray and work on yourself, you cannot make the other person stay.

This is why it is so important that couples both have a relationship with Christ. I mean a real relationship with Christ. Not merely the profession of faith and salvation; but the walk, the testimonies, the trials, the travail, the test, the victory, the witness and the leading of others to Christ. That's not too much to expect. Strive for those aforementioned experiences. Seek God for a partner and have those discussions about a true relationship with Christ. Thinking about divorce? Seek God and Counsel.

CHAPTER THIRTEEN

BEATING THE ODDS

"This is the day that the Lord has made, I will rejoice and be glad in it!"

Psalm 118:24

"Giving all glory and honor to God, praising Him for allowing me to see this day that I never dreamed I'd see! My 65th birthday! Thank you Lord! The Doctor told my mother to abort me, cause she wouldn't live to give birth. She went on a 7 day total fast, and praise God, she lived till I was 25 and 40 years later, I'm still here! Hallelujah! No weapon formed against me can prosper! I'm blessed and highly favored to be on the battlefield for my Lord!"

Lotus Thompson, California, USA

SECTION EIGHT
-LONELY BUT NOT ALONE-

CHAPTER FOURTEEN

WHEN LONELINESS ACHES

"You whom I have taken from the ends of the earth, and called from its farthest regions, and said to you. You are my servant, I have chosen you and have not cast you away: Fear not, for I am with you; be not dismayed, for I am your God. I will strengthen you, Yes, I will help you and uphold you with my righteous right hand."

Isaiah 41:9-10

I know that I am not the only one that feels terribly lonely at times. Plans don't pan out. Relationships are not what they appear to be. Yet you are the hardest working person you know with a heart bigger than...Texas. Then in the midst of what seems like a dry desert, there is a cool mist. Sort of a refreshing in your spirit that soothes your parched thoughts and cracked emotions. I have been set apart. I realized this in 2000, 16 years ago. I'm an anomaly. God wants my total submission and my sum is not the right answer. Hope I haven't lost you with my sublime. My point is, pay attention to that fraction of joy or light in that very dark place and follow it. It will surely sustain you. Whether you have accepted Him or not, He is there. See that flicker of light, it's The Savior, Jesus.

SECTION NINE
-BEING USED BY GOD-

CHAPTER FIFTEEN

IT'S A LIFESAVER

Approximately five years ago, I made 5 AM phone call to a friend that I met in Hawaii at my former my church. I had no idea why I called him out of the clear blue sky, as they say. I vaguely remembered waking up about 4 AM prior to my call to him with a heavy burden and began to pray however, I did not know what I was praying about. This phone call had confirmed why I was in prayer early that morning. He was baffled by my call and what a timely one it was. I'm so glad he answered the phone that one morning.

My dear friend Chris the other end of the line very distraught! I immediately sat straight up in bed so I can attend to my friend and listen intently. Chris was on his way to confront his wife about an affair. As he began to speak mostly with expletives, I urged him to pull over and calm down. As he pulled over, I listened to his sobbing for about

10 to 15 minutes while I prayed silently. Then I said, "my friend, God is with you I'm going to pray for you and I want you to give it over to Him." As he continued to sob, I began to pray and speak life into his life. Through the Holy Spirit, I began to speak about his purpose and the plan that God ultimately had for him. I have no idea how long the prayer lasted, but I began to witness the calming of his spirit.

After the talk and prayer, my friend thanked me and I told him now I know why I was up early that morning in prayer with a heavy burden, it was for him. As we ended the conversation, I told my friend that it was time for prayer and fasting and we committed to a time of prayer and fasting together for this specific situation. About two weeks later, my friend called me with a praise report stating that he and his wife had reconciled their differences and God was moving on behalf of their marriage. However, he also told me that on that day, he was on his way to kill his wife, then kill himself. In addition, he mentioned once he came to himself, he realized that he was parked in front of a police station. When he initially pulled over, he had not realized during that very trying time that he was directly across from a police station. To really give you an idea of how God had intervened on his behalf—although the enemy tried to destroy his life—he was a Chief of Police at the time. Just say wow! I know, look at God, Hallelujah!

Recently, in the past month or so, I spoke with him and reminded him of this event in his life. I told him it was going to be anonymously added to the devotional. He was happy for my success and all, but he proceeded to tell me what has transpired as a result of that very day. He told me that he and his wife not only sought counsel but for the first time in his life he finally dealt with who he was. He began to really work on himself and a deeper relationship with God. He stated, "Tammy, that prayer that day saved my life and was the catalyst to my ministry!"

What a dynamic testimony! This was a few years ago and even though his marriage eventually ended, his ministry began. He is now an ordained minister planted in a ministry where God is using him mightily! To God be ALL the glory! You never know when God is going to use you to save a life. Stay prayed up and follow the leading of the Holy Spirit. Amen!

CHAPTER SIXTEEN

PUTTING AN END TO SELFISHNESS

A few years ago I was working at Hospice as a Triage Nurse and very happy until some management issues arose. With these changes, the organization was in utter turmoil. While changes were being made, a new Director of Nursing offered me a position as a manager at our in-patient facility rather than the admin office where I was working at the time. I asked management to give me an opportunity to think about it and weigh the pro's and con's and they not only agreed, but encouraged me to do so.

I took time specifically in prayer regarding this position. I weighed the pro's and con's, I assessed the financial aspects and I just prayed for peace. I had no peace whatsoever about accepting the position and later that week I respectfully declined that position and decided to continue as the triage nurse. They...the Executive Director and Director of Nursing, seemed quite surprised and disappointed with my decision however, immediately offered the position to one of my colleagues.

Later that afternoon, the colleague who was offered the position contacted me to get some insight on the position and the reason I had declined the position. I frankly told her that I had no peace about accepting the position. She being a professing believer, asked me to explain. I stated simply, "I prayed and had no peace, therefore I declined the position." Our conversation ended and then the war began.

A few days later, management had a meeting and announced the new positions and yes, that colleague accepted that position. Lots of changes occurred and for me the biggest change was that they were removing me from admin and placing me on the floor at the in-patient facility and the colleague was now going to be my direct supervisor. Yes, my boss! Wow! I did not see that coming, a double-whammy! I was distraught and upset, but there was nothing I could do. Let me fast-forward. When I was transferred, I was now not even functioning as a LPN (Licensed Practical Nurse), I was functioning as a CNA (Certified Nursing Assistant). For those in the healthcare field, you will understand. A CNA is a caregiver who has some training and state board testing to prove competency. An LPN is a nurse with much more training who is able to function in the capacity of a supervisor in certain facilities and has a license to administer medications, treatments, injections, etc. I worked hard for that license and I also went back to school for my management degree and obtained a Bachelor's of Science in Health Administration many years prior to this position.

Needless to say, I was way over qualified to be functioning as a CNA. This was 2012 and I had not been a CNA since 1998. Go figure. I was upset and my new manager made sure I was assigned to a task to humiliate me. But here is when the big turnaround happened. One day on my shift, I was assigned an one-to-one case. This means I have to stay within arm's length of one patient for the entire shift. No relief except for lunch and to use the bathroom. Every Nurse, CNA, and caregiver dread having one-to-one shifts, but it is necessary for the patient. This particular patient, I will call him Bob, was agitated and a bit combative. This is one of the signs you see in Hospice shortly before a patient passes away. I won't get into the medical explanation, but it seemed to be close to the time that he would be dying. I assisted him throughout the day for the entire shift, and believe me the time was ticking by slowly. I was upset the entire shift until about an hour before my shift ended.

I got this check in my spirit and the Holy Spirit convicted me. I did not hear an audible voice, but my voice in my head prompted by God said, "Tammy, you have been here for an entire seven hours complaining about things not going your way while caring for a dying man. Are you dying, because you surely are not praying. All of this time you could have been praying for this man. Do you even know if he has accepted Jesus Christ as his Lord and Savior!?" Oh my word! How selfish of me! I had not prayed, I had not asked! Although he was quite incoherent, I had not done anything except complain. I only cared about me while this man was on his death bed. I immediately asked God for forgiveness and began to spend the next hour in prayer for Bob. The next day I was excited about my one-to-one shift. I had stopped being selfish and now my focus and agenda had changed. I walked into Bob's room and he was sitting straight up in bed. "Good morning, are you my nurse today? Mr. Bob startled me, I said, "Yes Mr. Bob, I am." Wow, I said to myself as I began to assist him.

Well, I had a chance to get to know Mr. Bob throughout that day. He was calm, coherent, and delightful. He didn't have much family, no children, was not married and his only living family member was a sister. I asked him about his experience with God and religion and he had no experience. Well, I shared the gospel (good news) about Christ and led Mr. Bob to Jesus that day!

Heaven was rejoicing, Hallelujah! What a profound moment in my history. Once I took my eyes off of my circumstances, I was able to be a blessing to Mr. Bob. God was now able to use me when I put an end to selfishness. It was a Friday afternoon when I led Mr. Bob to Christ. That Monday morning when I went into work with joy in my heart and ready for my shift, I had learned that Mr. Bob went on to be with the Lord on Saturday, that very next day after receiving Christ. I cried and rejoiced! Do you know what I did after that? Asked for another one-to-one shift and they gave it to me! Let me tell you, when I was not on one-to-one, I went to every room talking to every Hospice patient offering prayer. Many could not speak, some could only nod, but regardless I was praying for them and with them. I have no idea how many actually came to Christ besides Mr. Bob, but you know what? I learned a valuable lesson in my walk. I learned to stop complaining about my circumstances because I could have been on my death bed and without a Savior. So I put an end to selfishness and if my journey of evangelism had been stagnant, Mr. Bob's one -on-one brought it to the forefront and my proclamation of the gospel has never been the same. That should not only make you rejoice, but it should make you grab a cup of Tea and spend some Time with God!

"Go therefore and make disciples of all the nations, baptizing them in the name of the Father and of the Son and of the Holy Spirit, teaching them to observe all things that I have commanded you, and lo, I am with you always, even to the end of the age. Amen." **Matthew 28:19-20**

SECTION TEN
-FORGIVENESS-

CHAPTER SEVENTEEN

READY TO FORGIVE

Forgiveness does not have to be hard, you just do it because God continues to extend that forgiveness to you. If there is no apology, make forgiveness available anyway. Remember there is one who will never leave you or forsake you, so really you are not alone in this circumstance. Be the best you that you can be. Continue to grow daily and watch God move on your behalf even when it hurts, forgive anyway.

"For if you forgive men their trespasses, your heavenly Father will also forgive you. But if you do not forgive men their trespasses, neither will your Father forgive your trespasses."

Matthew 6:14-15

SECTION ELEVEN
-FREE YOUR MIND-

CHAPTER EIGHTEEN

THE BATTLE IS IN THE MIND

"We demolish arguments and every pretension that sets itself up against the knowledge of God, and we take captive every thought to make it obedient to Christ."

II Corinthians 10:5

You know what's so true? My former Pastor delivered a message stating that when we are concerned about something, we role play the events in our head, allow negative thoughts to sabotage the plan of God, predict our demise, then we carry it out like a pre-written script. But the truth is, if we give it to God, really give it to Him in the midst of our storm, he will tell the wind and waves to cease!

But in our heads we already play out the end and allow the enemy to get the victory. Sisters, tell the enemy that your role playing days are over! The battle is in the mind; take authority in Jesus name, Amen!

Make today victorious by casting your thoughts, cares, ideas, worries and issues to Almighty God. There is no place you would rather be than in His will. He already wrote the script. Allow God to use you until the end of your own Life Time movie.

MUSIC TO MY EARS

"Do not be anxious about anything, but in every situation, by prayer and petition, with thanksgiving present your request to God."

Philippians 4:6 (NIV)

Today, as I watched the devastation of the rain with no name invade Baton Rouge, I was thinking of my uncle, Arthur. Oh, how I miss him. It was like yesterday when Katrina hit almost 11 years to date that my uncle was rescued from the roof top of his home. Two days prior a man crossed his path with ax that he wanted to sell for $10.00. My uncle did not want to purchase it, but the guy was hustling I guess and my uncle bought the ax. It was the ax that saved his life. The same one he used to chop a hole into the ceiling to escape and later be rescued from the roof of his home.

Why music to my ears? Well, my uncle passed away in February of this year 2016 and I visited him almost every day for three weeks prior to him passing. There was one day in particular, my mom and I went together to visit my uncle. I usually go alone, pray with and for my uncle, then leave. This day my mom led the prayer. I had never heard her pray aloud before except for blessing the food. It was music to my ears! The earnestness and sincerity mixed with supplication and petition, I can't tell you as a daughter the pride and gratefulness I felt when I heard her pray! Knowing that my mom prays for me gives me so much strength. I knew she prayed for me but I just never heard her pray before until that day.

My sons have always heard me pray. To not hear me pray would be out of the norm. I taught them how to pray and poured the Word of God and the love of Christ into them their entire lives. My point is, 20 years plus of my prayers is wonderful, but those 2 minutes of hearing my mom pray aloud will last me a lifetime. I can only imagine what my sons must feel like when they hear me pray. Take the time to pray aloud with your children. You never know how those two minutes of love will impact their lives forever!

Ladies, not only are you fabulous, but phenomenal!

CATCHING UP ON MY "I LOVE YOU'S"

I grew up in a family that did not often say, "I love you", but love was evident. I must admit, I had not always felt loved but I love to love, if that makes sense. I've always loved all of my family, but now feel compelled to make it known.

I noticed as I was growing up and falling in love and acquiring great friends that I love dearly, I said I love you more and more with verbal expression, but not much to my family, not even my mother. I've realized that there are a number of reasons/excuses that I can come up with for not saying I love you, but it really doesn't matter when they are gone; it matters while they are here.

So as I reflect, re-evaluate, reminisce, I'm catching up, with my I love you's especially with my mom. Does she know...of course, but hearing it is golden. We have been through a lot, but the fact is, I love my mother and my family. So to family member, just know...Tanisha Crosby-Powell, Tamara Witherspoon Laymond, Gilda Crosby, Derrinesha White, Tara Jackson, Tonya White, Hilda Singleton, Gisele Jackson, Nicole Jackson, and all of my direct family. I love you!

Lisa Brown James, Tracye Gee-Lewis, Theresa McCaffety-Ellman, Latesha McCaffety, Seanna Laymond, Shelita LuvJesus Laymond, Carolyn Jenkins-Meekins, Harriette Bryant, Mary Robinson, Kathleen M. Butler, Cynthia M. Meekins, Christina Meekins, Erin Renee, Zenia Boswell, Denise Boswell Lord, Shelley Giles, and the whole former Way of Truth Family and former New Vision Christian Center Family, The Mount Lebanon Family and the Christ The King Family and currently the My Redeemer Missionary Baptist Church family and all of the folks I've known for years and too choked up right now to tag everyone, I love you!

Some I just met and adore, Jane JJ Johnson, Elena Artugue, Cristina Prudhomme, Julianne White, Carol Riley-Wilkerson, Betty Walker, Cindy Abbay-Lugo, Sue Glenn, Toni Miller, Julie Bodle, Judie Zanter Book, OMG so many more of you, I love you! Everyone in my phenomenal women Facebook group that I have met and broke bread with, had coffee with, shared laughs and cries with, I love you!

Some I have never met or haven't seen in forever Laura Wichman, Lynette Jones, Tina Jones, so many others, I love you! Please if I didn't mention your name it's only because I could not tag you in my group at the time. Chef Natasha Butler and Chef Wendy Weber, I love you.

To all the men in my life: Jesus Christ my Lord and Savior; my Uncles, the late Arthur, Alvin, Anthony and Bobby White. May you all rest in heaven, I love you. To my uncle August White, I love you. My grandfather Arthur White, Sr. I miss and love you. I can go on and on, but my heart can't take it right now. Don Meyers, you encouraged me over and over to write and I'm finally doing it, I love you and I hate that I did not finish it before you left this earth far too soon, rest in heaven my friend, I love you.

I have so many more I love you's. Wait before I end, Kenneth Ervin Mitchell aka Mitch, I love you my friend. You have been there for me and my son's in such a literal sense, I cannot begin to put into words how much I appreciate you.

You stepped in as a positive male figure during those crucial teenage years for my sons. That is priceless and you have always been there for my "single mom" meltdowns. I love you dearly and God knew that I needed a true friend, he sent you.

Pastor Offie S. Sheard III, I love you my friend. You always supported my ministry from the beginning. Thank you. I will always need you, never forget that. You were a role model for my sons and I watched the respect they had for you because of the love you poured into them. You have always been there for me. Again, I love you.

Pastor Audwin Meekins, I love you. Always encouraging no matter what. Pastor Floyd Robinson, thank you sir for unwavering servitude like I have never ever seen, I love you. Pastor Brian Clark aka Poppa C, you loved me back to life and had my back. You counseled me out of darkness. For that, I love you and your wife Beth. To my spiritual Poppa James L. Giles, you left a few short months ago. You laid the foundation for my Christian walk. You showed me love, prayer, fasting, how to study, resilience, how to examine myself, passion, trust, belief, faith, and how to be a respectful woman of God. You restored my faith in men after a troubled childhood of emotional abuse. You taught me when to stand and when to sit. I love you. Rest in heaven. You inspired my authorship. Thank you.

Last but not least, thank you S.D. Horton for inspiring me to write and helping it come to fruition. I love you my friend.

Just know, I love you all. You are all special to me...all who have supported me with this book and even those who haven't.

Mom, Lenora White Jones, again I love you!

MEET A COUPLE OF
PHENOMENAL WOMEN

JANE JOHNSON

Devoted Mother, Nurse, Friend and Domestic Violence Survivor

Photo provided by Jane Johnson

Approximately 6 years ago on Jane's birthday, Jane's life was turned upside down. I had the pleasure of meeting Jane and we became friends almost instantly over lunch at a training we both attended. While becoming acquainted, Jane he disclosed to me that her husband was deceased. Noting that she was very young I asked her how he died if she didn't mind talking about it. She stated that he had committed suicide. My background in mental health helped me understand depression and how that sort of thing can happen. I expressed my condolences while feeling that love she had for her husband. Then she disclosed the shocking news about the attempted murder/suicide event that had taken place. I was puzzled, I saw the love on her face and heard the love and adoration for her husband in her voice. But, he tried to kill her in front of her boys as I gasped not saying a word. It was the forgiveness that got my attention, I immediately knew that she was phenomenal and asked her to speak at one of my events.

Jane spoke at my event in February 2015 and walked a group of women through 14 years of her life of abuse like you would never believe. There was a hush in the room while she spoke, but then you would hear sighs, weeping, and some had to leave because it was too much. The vivid description of such horrific abuse, yet she still celebrates his birthday with their three sons and still professes her love for him while being thankful that she survived. Phenomenal woman she is!

CONNIE SCHILTZ

Dedicated Mother, Friend, and Sister in the Lord,
as well as a Brain Tumor Survivor

Left to Right: Tammy White, Connie Schiltz, and Theresa Ellman

Photo provided by Restless Wings Photography

Approximately 6 years ago, this beautiful lady in the center was undergoing an operation for a benign brain tumor that would forever change her life. At that time, she did not have a relationship with God but now makes a joke about God getting her attention with this tumor. She refers to herself as "hard-headed" while she is continuously striving to maintain her life and health after a traumatic experience.

Her survival of the brain tumor is only one thing that makes her phenomenal; she is also a live organ donor. She so happened to be a match for her oldest child and only daughter Tiffany who needed a kidney transplant in her 20s some years go.

Connie loves life, music, and she loves to dance. She has so much life in her. You would not believe her age and that she has had brain surgery and living with one kidney. While I won't disclose her age, take it from me she looks 20 years younger! Another phenomenal woman for sure.

Enjoy Chapter 1 from my book upcoming book
HIDDEN TREASURE
COMING SOON...END OF SUMMER 2017

HIDDEN TREASURE

*How One Woman Finally Exposes Her Trauma
to find the Gem Within.*

Tammy L. White

CHAPTER 1

A RUBY IS WORTH MORE THAN A PENNY

As tears ran down my face, I could not believe this was happening again. He laid to my left on his back with his private parts bulging as I felt some wetness. Using his left hand to stroke his manhood, he used his right hand to play with my innocence. I was in this situation again as mama was off to a long hard day of work without a clue. I had to be only eight years old at the time.

This sick game became a normal routine, no matter what time of the day it was. My soon to be step-dad Rick, found time to have his Ruby-fix, on a consistent basis. "Ruby come here, I got something to tell you." It was sickening.

I remember like it all like it was yesterday. My mama had a big smile on her face as she patted the bed next to her as a gesture for me to sit down. Rick was laying his overweight behind across the bed as usual. He was a tall, large man who had a bald spot at the center of his head along with a shabby mustache and a devious smile and flashing gold teeth. He was an independent business owner and a dedicated member and leader at a local and now very large church in New Orleans.

Mama's smile haunts me to this very day because Rick would be a bigger challenge for me after she dropped the bomb. "I want to let you know that Rick and I are getting married!" The excitement in her voice caused an earthquake in my little fragile body. Every cell in my body began to fade; I instantly began to die inside. I don't know how else to explain it. Just a cold and dark feeling and I was scared.

Like some sort of a normal reflex, tears began to flow down my cheeks. Crying had released so much pain in my hurtful, troubled life that it became second nature. Little did I know that my cries would keep me alive to see many more years, it was my outlet. Mama seemed disturbed by my tears before saying, "I hope those are happy tears?" I just nodded and left the room. There was nothing for me to do, I was 12 years old and had become this man's nasty little secret and he had me as his side dish whenever he felt like it. He would have me as seconds after feasting at the table with such gluttony. He was a greedy man in every sense of the word. He was charming, so he put up a great facade and his demons would torture me for a long time little did I know.

So that day came, mama and Rick were married on what seemed to be the coldest day of winter ever in The Big Easy. Mama talks about it being a sign not to marry Rick; that's what she would say years after they divorced. You know New Orleans folk can be superstitious, but hard-headed at the same time. Between stepping on the cracks in the sidewalks that would surely "break your mama's back," or spitting on the broom if it touched your feet, would keep you from going to jail. People just would go overboard with that stuff. Nevertheless, the wedding took place and there I was witnessing the whole thing.

Being Rick's step daughter wasn't all bad I guess, from a helpless kid's point of view. He found time to be a family man. He would take me and my little sister to WWF wrestling matches every Monday night at the auditorium in Louis Armstrong Park. He also loved to eat as I mentioned, so he took us to Showbiz Pizza, kind of like the now Chuck E. Cheese. Kids loved that place and he would portray and present himself as that perfect family man. Providing financially and spending quality family time was his prop for a functional family setting; it was like a screen-play.

I found myself enjoying those times trying to forget about the 3am wake up visits by Rick while he breathes his nasty breath on me and sweating while taking care of himself right next to me. Sick bastard! I was a kid and I was caught in his web of perversion and was clueless to how this would affect me today! Clueless, but God had a plan for Ruby that's still unfolding today. My mama and sister seemed happy most of the time, so I surely was not going to cause any problems. I never told anyone about Rick until I was 25 years old. I vowed to go to my grave with that pain and Rick's deep dark secret until God stepped in. That's when life really began for me. I had been dead for so many years; finally, the resurrection of Ruby! Ruby...once a pebble, not as valuable as a penny...became priceless. What freedom! However, it's take years to finally realize my worth. Years!

Tammy is a New Orleans native who spent the last 23 years in the Seattle area. She is the mother of two exceptional young men ages 24 and 22 years old; Frederick Bell, Jr. and Te'ron J. Bell, who reside in Seattle, WA. Tammy has been in women's ministry for 15 years and encouraging women from all walks of life. She is the founder of an organization for young women G.E.M.S. (Grace Empowering Many Souls) which inspired her to write the testimony of her own life of hardship, depression, abuse, and triumph. She encourages others to embrace their true life story while experiencing the sufficient grace of God, (II Corinthians 12:9-10). Tammy is also the owner and founder of The FooDivaS along with her best friend Theresa Ellman who resides in Siversdale, WA. As the owner of the FooDivaS and Chef's Aid, LLC, she travels throughout the country ministering to women while promoting Chefs at her Phenomenal Women Events. She provides a platform for women to share their heart and story as they break bread and enjoy cuisine from the best Chefs in the country.

Chef's Aid

Supportive Chef Services

Chef's Aid

Chef's Aid renders support in the follow areas:

- Customized logos
- Customized menus for your client's special events
- Customized catering menus
- Event bookings & administrative assistance
- Bookings for festivals
- Marketing for private & public events
- Discount cards and promotions to solicit more clients
- Office party and professional bookings
- Social media monitoring and managing
- Market research for target audiences
- Hands on assistance for events
- Website creation (coming soon)
- Flyers & brochures to market any event

www.ChefsAid.org

chefsaidandconsulting@gmail.com